30 Day PRAYER JOURNALING

Building Your Prayer Life and Discovering Your True Identity

To Rachel:

Thank you for your support! May God continue to bless you and heaven shine upon you!

Blessings,
Melissa

30 Day PRAYER JOURNALING

Building Your Prayer Life and Discovering Your True Identity

Melissa Wells

30 DAY PRAYER JOURNALING

Published by Purposely Created Publishing Group™

Copyright © 2018 Melissa Wells

All rights reserved.

No part of this book may be reproduced, distributed or transmitted in any form by any means, graphics, electronics, or mechanical, including photocopy, recording, taping, or by any information storage or retrieval system, without permission in writing from the publisher, except in the case of reprints in the context of reviews, quotes, or references.

Printed in the United States of America

ISBN: 978-1-947054-80-6

Special discounts are available on bulk quantity purchases by book clubs, associations and special interest groups. For details email: sales@publishyourgift.com or call (888) 949-6228. For information logon to: www.PublishYourGift.com

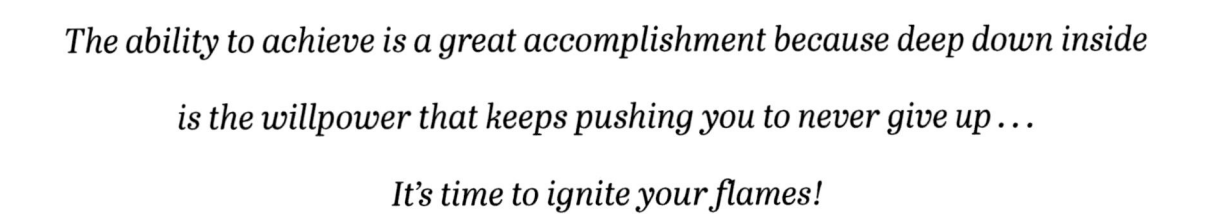

The ability to achieve is a great accomplishment because deep down inside

is the willpower that keeps pushing you to never give up...

It's time to ignite your flames!

DEDICATION

I would like to dedicate this, my first book, to my beloved mother, Emma Jane Wells, who is no longer with me. It was my mother who always inspired me to reach for the stars and for my dreams. She was the one who would always encourage me to continue and to never give up, no matter how big the problem or how hard the circumstances. I can still hear the words of my mother, telling me "you can do it!" She was always there to support me and make me feel larger than life. Mom, I know you are smiling down from heaven, rejoicing because you have been with me through my ups and downs and with me now as I am writing this dedication to you; your legacy will never die. Thank you for raising me and being my example of a virtuous woman; I have become what you have planted, your beautiful rose.

Love you!

Table of Contents

Acknowledgments xi

Foreword xiii

Introduction 1

Opening Prayer 7

    Day 1: The Forms of Prayer 9

    Day 2: Questions 13

    Day 3: Consecration 16

    Day 4: Free Indeed 19

    Day 5: Fasting 22

    Day 6: Attacks 25

    Day 7: Getting Ready 28

    Day 8: Stages 31

    Day 9: Discovery 35

    Day 10: Ready Your Weapons 38

    Day 11: Stormy Weather 41

    Day 12: Things Going Wrong 44

Day 13: Why 47

Day 14: Your Result 50

Day 15: Halfway There 53

Day 16: I Am 56

Day 17: No Doubt 59

Day 18: In Your DNA 62

Day 19: The Power of Your Words 65

Day 20: Fret Not 68

Day 21: Forming a Habit 71

Day 22: Day of Reflection 74

Day 23: What's Your ID? 77

Day 24: Trust 81

Day 25: Opportunity 84

Day 26: Plans 87

Day 27: The Message 90

Day 28: Perfect Timing 93

Day 29: Sharing the Journey 96

Day 30: The Next Level 99

Conclusion 103

About the Author 107

Acknowledgments

I would first like to thank my Lord and Savior for allowing me to be his chosen vessel in helping his people build their firm foundation and solid prayer life.

Secondly, I give thanks to my beautiful children, Raven and Desmond, who have encouraged me to continue and supported me along the way; you are my personal cheerleaders! I love you both so very much.

To my family and friends, thank you for your love and support along the way, which helped me in completing this book. You were always there to push me and offer advice.

A very special thanks to my friend Rick J. Lewis. Words cannot express my gratitude for your unwavering love and for the support you have shown. You have been in my corner since day one and have never left. I thank you for being genuine.

Foreword

Have you ever been asked who are you? Did you have to think about your response? Did you hesitate, or did you give the generic response––your name? How important is it to know who you really are, your true, God-given identity, to know your worth, to know your purpose in life? Just take a look around you. Watch the daily news, walk through your neighborhood, or listen to a friend, and you will discover that there is a dire need in the hearts of people for value and significance in the world today. It is not paramount only to a certain age group, or a certain segment of the population, or a certain status in life. It is universal, worldwide.

We all want to know who we are and why we exist. This is an inherent, deep-rooted desire. Many answers have been given to these questions: Why am I here? What is my purpose? Do I have significance? Can I make a difference? But the one significant, life-changing answer can only be discovered by spending whole-hearted, dedicated, devoted time in prayer with the Lord.

Melissa Wells takes you on an amazing journey in this book, *30 Day Prayer Journaling: Building Your Prayer Life and Discovering Your True Identity*, giving guidance and instructions each day. You won't feel alone on this journey. It is a well-traveled path and it is strategically designed by God. All along the way, there are empowering thoughts to keep you, the reader, focused and on track each day.

It is amazing when the Lord chooses a vessel and puts his stamp of approval on that person for his glory and for the health and welfare of his people—physically, spiritually, emotionally, and in many other ways. However, I am not surprised at the gifts and talents the Holy Spirit is manifesting in the life of this woman of God. I can recall my first close-up and personal encounter with Melissa. She was experiencing a most difficult life-changing situation in her marriage. I felt honored that she would trust me with something so personal and heartbreaking. I saw her brokenness but also her strong, determined resolve not to be destroyed by it. Our time in counsel and prayer was valuable, but her continued persistence in prayer was key to her renewed discovery of what God called her to be and do. She is actively fulfilling that call and reaching out to you through this book.

Melissa Wells has captured the heart of those who so desire to know and experience all of their worth and potential in God in their lifetime. Through her own experiences, good and bad, the Holy Spirit has birthed in her this treasure of devotions to assist in building, rebuilding, or enhancing a sustained relationship with God through prayer, fasting, worship, and praise. We have heard the old adage, "experience is the best teacher." I am not sure if it is the best, but it is most certainly a great teacher. Though a first-time writer, Melissa Wells is no stranger to God and the value of consistent, fervent prayer. It is evident she is truly "abiding under the shadow of the Almighty," and he is her "dwelling place" (Psalms 91:1, 84:1).

The way is paved in this book with a roadmap of thought-provoking statements that will move you toward a greater prayer life and a discovery of your true identity:

- "Ignite the flame in you."
- "Stop feeding your problems and start believing your God."
- "Don't let your problem bury you; bury your problem instead."
- "No doubt, keep Satan out!"

You will find that many of these powerful expressions will encourage and inspire hope in your quest for a greater relationship with God through your prayer life. Melissa's fervency to see you walking in the fullness of your potential and fulfilling your divine purpose is quite evident in this book.

Melissa Wells has traveled this road and she knows the way, but her journey continues toward greater things, as yours will also. Thirty days. Take the challenge. Start your journey. Stay on track to greater things.

Rev. Betty L. Young
Associate Pastor
Christian Life Church
Bible Teacher/Educator
Counselor/Mentor

Introduction

It wasn't until I was in my thirties that God spoke to me and revealed to me my gift. You see, all of us have gifts—and a choice of whether we listen to the voice of God or to our own voice. Although God revealed to me my gift and calling, my purpose on this earthly realm, it wasn't until I was well over forty that I began to operate in it. It wasn't until I was staring defeat in the face—dealing with the fear of losing everything, the struggles that come with low self-esteem, and the uncertainty of not having your life in your own control and not being prepared to deal with the curve balls that life throws at you—that I began to listen.

I was not prepared to encounter the curve ball of being divorced—the capital D! I was in a low place, feeling defeated and making bad decisions; in a state of disbelief, all I could do was wonder how it had come to such a point. I dwelt on the whys that we ask ourselves at such times. I felt ashamed, with my pride not wanting anyone to know. These were all emotions that I was feeling; my life seemed like a rollercoaster that was never going to stop. But God, I must say that again, but God! He was there for me every step of the way. He comforts me in my distress; as he stated in Matthew 5:4 (NIV), "Blessed are those who mourn, for they will be comforted."

To those of you who are reading this book: never allow yourself to face any type of struggle, pain, or hurt alone. You will not make it! You must tell someone, because you will not be able to function alone; your willpower is not that strong. Go to the one who is higher than all. Go to the one who is omniscient, all-knowing, the one who is omnipresent, everywhere at the same time. Go to God, the source of our life. He is the source of everything you need in this lifetime, for he has already prepared plans for you during this lifetime and after. As it says in John 14:3 (NIV): "And if I go and prepare a place for you, I will come back and take you to be with me that you also may be where I am."

God, who is the Alpha and the Omega, knows your beginning and your ending. Although we have heard this and know this, we still seem to face life with self-doubt and fear. We know who God is, we hear of the miraculous things he has done and continues to do, yet we still have unbelief about whether or not God will help us. We ask ourselves the *wills*... Will I be able to accomplish all of my dreams and goals in life? Will I be able to become a famous athlete? Doctor? Singer? Will I have the money to go to school and get my degree? Will I get the promotion? Will I become an entrepreneur? Will I become an investor? Will I be rich? Will I be healed from this sickness in my body? Will I be able to afford this car or home? So many questions we ask ourselves every single second—yes! I said second, because we always have at least one, or even more than one, thoughts of doubt or unbelief in our minds, and these doubts haunt us daily.

Today, May 28, 2017, I got up this morning from my bed around 8:45 a.m. and God spoke to me, saying: "Get up and get a pen and pad and begin to write." These pages that you are reading are from the author of your faith; as it says in Hebrews 12:2 (KJV), we should always be "looking unto Jesus, the author and finisher of our faith; who for the joy that was set before him endured the cross, despising the shame, and is set down at the right hand of the throne of God." He has your life already orchestrated. He knows the plans he has for you, as in Jeremiah 29:11. God wants to take you to a place where even your thoughts will amaze you; he wants you to be a witness to greatness; he wants you to be able to walk upon this earth and perform greater works.

God's plan for your life is for you to be great! For you to serve and for you to be his voice, the vessel for his works. God wants for you to look only to him and become fearless in your mind, body, and soul. He wants for you to have a determined, made-up mind, such as his servant Job, who said: "Though he slay me, yet will I trust in him: but I will maintain mine own ways before him" Job 13:15 (KJV). What fascinates me is that Job had a made-up mind that, even if he lost everything, he would still trust God. He would not waver in his faith. He knew that if he did, he would allow the enemy, Satan, to creep into his heart and mind. The very moment you doubt your belief, that's when you give Satan the keys to access your mind.

Once Satan has the key to your mind, he recalls the things of your past; he never speaks about your future because he is not privy to that information. He knows only what he can see; he is weak! He has no power, and we give Satan way too much credit. He goes around like a roaring lion seeking whom he may devour. He is a pretender! He is not the Lion of Judah. He is a pretender!

God the Father knows about your life. He knows your thoughts when you wake up in the morning and when you lie down at night. He knows the plan of your day before your head even lifts from the pillow; he knows you! As Jeremiah 1:5 (NIV) says, "Before I formed you in the womb I knew you, before you were born I set you apart; I appointed you as a prophet to the nations."

Let that grab hold of your spirit as it did mine. There are no surprises to God! Nothing we can say or do surprises him. He knows. God's plan for your life is to set you apart; you are not like any other creature, you have been set apart; you are fearfully and wonderfully made in the eyes of God. The psalmist says in Psalm 139:14 (NIV): "I praise you because I am fearfully and wonderfully made; your works are wonderful, I know that full well." You will be like no other; you are unique. You might look alike—twins, triplets, etc.—but you are unique; your very fingerprints have a different pattern than anyone else's. They tell the story of who you are. Your fingerprints describe and have your true identity. Although you might want to be like the most popular girl, boy, friend, or celebrity, you can't and will never be like anyone else, because that's not who God made you to be; we are our own unique individual.

The closest way to becoming like that person you admire is through pretending, and we know that if you go around pretending to be like someone else, it only leads you down the path of the adversary, Satan. He tries and tries and tries to be like God, but he never will be. And if you have the same mindset, wanting to live in someone else's shadow, then you will not really get to live out the life God has designed for you, not be able to find out who you really are through discovering your identity.

In order to identify who you are, your hidden talents, the gift or gifts God has for your life, you must first spend time with our Father. He is the creator of who we are and the source of your life and mine. If you want to discover and know the true you, then you must get a personal relationship with God. I am not only talking about spending time with God in your prayer times; that is good, but in order to discover you must do research. It took more than prayer for Job to be able to keep the faith in the midst of losing everything, yet he did not break, but instead persevered and never doubted God. Job never doubted because of the relationship he developed with God. We can never doubt God because he has proven so much to us, but the saying "we are our own worst critics" is true; we doubt ourselves when we are unstable and do not know our own strengths.

We need to have the perspective and mindset of God. Once you have changed your mindset, you are allowing God to show you all the things he has ordained for you. Remember, though, that these things might be different from the thoughts held by your family, friends, coworkers, significant others, pastors, or teachers, or by anyone else who has had an influence in your life and has, one way or the other, had a huge impact on your decisions. When God has given us one direction, too often we listen to the voice of reason and take a different direction instead. We need to get to a place of only listening and following the voice of God, and to remain steadfast and not be so easily influenced or persuaded.

This book will be a road map to the personal growth and development of your prayer life with God. During the next thirty days, through devotions, prayer, meditation, fasting, reading, and worshipping, you will get to a place where you can discover the God that lives within you. You will begin to unleash the channels to God's holy throne. I must first warn you that this discovery and journey will not be easy. There will be all types of spiritual attacks heading your way; there will be fear, doubt, pain, betrayal, envy, malice, and a time of loneliness; but when these attacks come, just continue to keep your head up, because you are doing the right thing. You are discovering your identity and your strength; you are unlocking and learning not only about our Father, but also, and most importantly, yourself and what you are made of.

Rome was not built in a day; this is also true with you in finding out your true identity. It takes time, prayer, fasting, consecration, worship, saying no, and spending a lot of time with God to discover your true being and the power that lies within you. Commitment and consistency are the keys that will both keep you going while completing this journey and prevent you from feeling that everything is against you. Being a Christian and living a wholesome life require sacrifices. The price that you are willing to pay reveals to you another level of your identity. You will not be in this walk alone. God your Father will be with you always; he will never leave you for he calls you friend.

Discover what you are made of; discover your ability to speak of things that are not yet as though they already are. Speak the words of life over yourself and speak with the authority that you possess. After the thirty days of this journey, if you have not found your true identity the reason is one of two things: you either stopped searching and became weary or you chose not to believe. When you discover your identity and find that you know, there is nothing in this world that can stop you! Let's begin with a prayer of commitment, purification, and sanctification unto the God of all gods!

Opening Prayer

Heavenly Father, the one who created heaven and earth, I vow to you this day, and for the remaining thirty days, to pour out my spirit to you. I vow to surrender those things that have been hindering me in having a closer relationship with you, those things that have been keeping me from discovering my true identity in you. I commit myself to spending my mornings and evenings in prayer through worshipping, fasting, reading, meditating, and praising. I commit myself to giving up those things that will distract me or cause me to feel exhausted or tired. I commit myself to continuing to push through the hurt and pain. I know that attacks and trials will come, but I am persuaded that nothing will stop me from discovering my true identity and building a more solid and intimate relationship with you. I know that no good thing will you withhold from me if I seek after you.

I pledge on this day, _____, to surrender myself unto you; use me as you see fit and teach me your ways. I know you have set me apart as a prophet to the nations. I am called to greatness because it's in my DNA. Help me to grab hold of my true calling on this earth so that I may have all of your plans fulfilled for my life. I sanctify and purify my spirit to you, God. Allow me to witness discoveries every day during this thirty-day journey. Let me be the living testimony that—as you promise in Matthew 6:33—if we seek you, seek the kingdom of God and your righteousness, all good things shall be added unto us. I want to know the things that shall be added unto me.

I thank you for equipping my spirit, mind, and body to deal with what lies ahead. I thank you for the spirit that will guide me to never give up but instead be always ready. Father, the journey begins in less than twenty-four hours, but the course will be a lifetime, one that will be filled with the love, joy, and happiness that can only come from you.

I shall keep in mind the saying: "The race is not given to the swift nor the battle to the strong, but to the one who endures to the end." Amen.

I pray for you, you pray for me, as iron sharpens iron; thus will God the Father deliver us. Stay the course, even when you feel like you are falling and losing your way; remember that God is with you at all times.

Let's begin this journey through *30 Day Prayer Journaling: Building Your Prayer Life and Discovering Your True Identity*.

Day 1

The Forms of Prayer

Prayer comes in many different forms, just like how communication can be either written or verbal. For prayer, these forms can be speaking out loud, singing, dancing, or even writing out thoughts. For me, I do them all. The more you communicate with God, the more he talks back, and he speaks using the same channels as I describe above. So when you think you are not hearing from God, it's not that he is not speaking, it's that you might not know the many forms he is communicating through because of your traditional mindset.

Many of us were told as children to say our prayers out loud so God could hear us. And today, we follow this same mindset into our adulthood, that this is the only way to communicate with God so he can hear us and vice versa. We need to first change our mindset. Once we change this mindset, it will allow us to not only pay more attention to detail but also to listen a lot more.

We will find ourselves listening to the lyrics of a song, then just stomping to the beat, dancing to the Lord; we will find ourselves listening when we pray out loud, then just saying words that we recall being taught as children, as teenagers, or even as adults, giving praise to the Lord.

Prayer can even be silent. Pause to listen. Some days I spend hours in prayer, and it's nothing but silent. But it's okay, because even when you think God isn't saying anything, he always brings a word. It might not be at that moment, it might be days after your prayer of silence, but it comes. God always responds to your prayers; you must discover his ways of communicating with you. Remember, it's not always going to be like the way we communicate with each other. His ways and thoughts are higher than ours. As God tells us in Isaiah 55:8–9 (KJV): "For my thoughts are not your thoughts, neither are your ways my ways, saith the Lord. For as the heavens are higher than the earth, so are my ways higher than your ways, and my thoughts than your thoughts."

What will your prayer be? How will you discover your true identity? What will you say? Speak from the heart, speak from within, let God know your thoughts; after all, nothing surprises God, he is all-knowing.

When the disciples asked Jesus to teach them how to pray, he said:

Our Father in heaven, hallowed be your name, your kingdom come, your will be done, on earth as it is in heaven. Give us today our daily bread. And forgive us our debts, as we also have forgiven our debtors. And lead us not into temptation, but deliver us from the evil one. Matthew 6:9b–13 (NIV)

It's not a long, drawn-out prayer, but it is a prayer of humility, of humbling yourself and acknowledging God the Father. In it, you also acknowledge your temptations and ask for forgiveness of your sins and your debtors; those who have wronged you and the things you have done wrong, you must forgive.

The prayer speaks about the life that we live. We are living in a world where there is sin and debt; everything is paid with a price! There is a cost to everything that we want in this lifetime, and we must often go into debt to get it. That's the way of the world. Satan has us all fooled! You won't discover the truth until you change your mindset; you should not be in debt, that's why Jesus says to forgive our debts as we forgive our debtors. As Proverbs 22:7 (NIV) says: "The rich rule over the poor, and the borrower is slave to the lender." It's a trap! God died on the cross and paid everything in full. God does not want us to walk around in sin, buried in debt. The modern system has us thinking that, in order to get nice things, we must go into debt. We become slaves to the lender—because you never repay only what you borrow, you always owe more—while this world works to keep us forever in debt.

Once you begin to not only pray the Lord's Prayer but to listen to and study the words that you say, you will begin to renew your mind. Begin to pray the Lord's Prayer and meditate on it line by line until you achieve understanding of the words that Jesus taught his disciples. Anything that God gives us teaches a lesson. God does not want you to get only the concept, but also the lesson behind it. Let your prayer today begin with the Lord's Prayer; ponder on and research why he chose those words. What's the meaning of the prayer? And what lesson is in it?

Keywords of destruction: sin, temptation, debt, debtors, evil.

Keywords of reassurance: deliver, your will be done, your kingdom come, our daily bread.

The next page begins your journaling of your prayer to God for day one.

Journal Your Prayer

Day 1

Today's date:_____

Day 2

Questions

Continue with the Lord's Prayer as you pray. In fact, let this be your introduction to the beginning of your prayer time with God. He deserves and desires our praise and worship. Open up the channels to God's holy throne through your acknowledgment of God the Father and who he really is, and then move on to your mistakes and confession. Confession is good for the soul; it releases your doubt of God not loving you or forgiving you. Remember, he told the disciples they should pray in a certain way and then told them the Lord's Prayer. Therefore, he already knew that they were going to make mistakes, mess up, and sin. He knew and knows, "for all have sinned and fall short of the glory of God" Romans 3:23 (NIV).

God's grace and his mercy have kept us and continue to keep us. Never have fear and doubt in your heart that God doesn't care or will never forgive you, for there is nothing you can do that will stop God from loving you. Today, go a little deeper in your prayer time with God. Begin to inquire about who he really is; ask the questions you want to ask of him. It's okay to ask God a question. We at times second-guess ourselves because of what our parents and Sunday school teachers have taught us. We are to never question God! You are not questioning God, what you are doing is simply asking God a question. God, again, knows all things, so what better source to go to than the God that has all of the answers?

I did not discover this until I took the time to begin to search and ask more of God, to ask what the plans were that he had for my life. What was my purpose and who was I? I want you to toss those old methods of thought out of your mind; if God didn't want us to know or ask of him, why would he say you have not because you ask not? We don't ask the real questions we want to, we beat around the bush. Understanding God and erasing all of the things we have been taught is hard. Habits are very hard to break, but through communicating with God and getting to know him, you will soon erase those traditional ways and do things God's way!

Now, please don't misinterpret me when I say it's okay to ask God a question. Yes, you can ask questions, but remember that you are not questioning his authority or his power over what he can do, for we know that there is nothing too hard for God! "I am the LORD, the God of all mankind. Is anything too hard for me?" (Jeremiah 32:27, NIV). I often find myself, in my prayer time, asking God questions, for if I am going to discover who I am, my true identity, it must start with researching and getting to know the source, God. You must ask questions to find out who you are; don't be afraid, God loves to hear from you, so go ahead and ask away.

The next page begins your journaling of your prayer to God for day two.

Journal Your Prayer

Day 2

Today's date:_____

_____
_____
_____
_____
_____
_____
_____
_____
_____
_____
_____
_____
_____
_____

Day 3

Consecration

You are praying the Lord's Prayer and asking questions about your true identity. Now it's time to go a little deeper. I know you're probably wondering, how much deeper can I go? With God, there are no limits. Limits are off when it comes to God! Let's begin to consecrate. Consecrate yourself to God; it's time to set yourself apart. Not only say it but do it! Allow yourself to be fully used by God. In consecrating yourself to God the Father, Son, and Holy Spirit, the Trinity, you are not only making a sacrifice, but also making a bold statement—that you are willing to give up everything to get in a deeper relationship with God despite your shortcomings or failures.

When consecrating, anoint yourself with oil and confess your sin before the Holy Spirit. Participate in Communion, taking the representations of the body and blood of Christ. Give God your heart and your all. Pray like your life depends on it. Don't be afraid. Go before God, putting yourself on the line, and cherish God, remembering all that he has done for you in sending his only begotten Son to die for our sin. Release yourself entirely to him, withholding nothing back.

Dedicate yourself back to him in such a way:

Purge me oh God! I want to be made whole again. I want to be made free from all sins, doubts, and debts. I want to be made free! Cleanse my mind from all negative thoughts. Cleanse my body from all habits of sin. Cleanse my soul and remove all bondage. I am no longer bound but set free!

Only you know what to ask God to deliver you from. Pour out your heart and be not afraid. God can and will set you free from bad habits, guilt, shame, and addictions. Consider God's command of consecration:

You shall anoint Aaron and his sons, and consecrate them, that they may serve me as priests. And you shall say to the people of Israel, "This shall be my holy anointing oil throughout your generations. It shall not be poured on the body of an ordinary person, and you shall make no other like it in composition. It is holy, and it shall be holy to you." Exodus 30:30–32. (ESV)

Consecration Prayer:

Heavenly Father, I come to you today to consecrate myself to you with this oil, which serves as a symbol of cleansing. I anoint my eyes for you to allow me to see beyond my physical vision, to see instead the spiritual vision of my future and the plans you have for me. I anoint my hands to serve in any capacity that you would allow me to work. With clean hands, I vow to be a vessel called by you to serve in the spiritual role of healing by the laying on of hands. I anoint my feet to walk the treacherous paths to deliver and reach your people, spreading the Gospel of Jesus Christ. I anoint my ears to be an active listener to your voice that will allow me to follow your plans and not my plans. Finally, I anoint my mouth as a vocal instrument in spreading and carrying out the Word of God.

The next page begins your journaling of your prayer to God for day three.

Journal Your Prayer

Day 3

Today's date:_____

_____
_____
_____
_____
_____
_____
_____
_____
_____
_____
_____
_____
_____
_____

Day 4

Free Indeed

WOW! I can only imagine how you are feeling right now. For me, I felt that the weight of the world was lifted off of me. It was a moment of serenity. I felt peace and tranquility, no longer wanting to hide or keep from speaking to God because of my sins, but instead actually crying out to him and truly knowing that God has forgiven me for all past mistakes. No longer getting caught up in man's thinking or the way this world is operated. No longer being afraid of being judged or having a care in the world for what folk say or think about me. Knowing that I am more than a conqueror, for "in all these things we are more than conquerors through him that loved us" Romans 8:37 (KJV).

In order for you to develop an intimate relationship with God, you must know God, and in order to know him, you must communicate with God freely. Having the freedom to speak your mind to God is exactly where God wants you to be. In my prayer time before I started this journaling of prayers, when I prayed, I was just finding great words to say. I did not pour out my heart or my feelings to God. I was afraid to talk to God. I didn't know what to say until I began to study the Word of God, pray more, and believe in what I was praying.

Today you overcome through the blood of Jesus Christ, just as Moses and the people of Israel overcame the army of Pharaoh and David overcame Goliath the Giant. You have been forgiven of all of your guilt, your shame, and your past mistakes. You must know that, no matter what the past holds, it's just that—the past!

You must no longer look back on your mistakes, but instead, as the Father has forgiven you, you must forgive yourself. Rid yourself of the pain and remember that you are free, as it says in John 8:36 (KJV): "So if the Son sets you free, you will be free indeed."

Whenever you feel like you are being haunted by your past, remember this scripture and speak it out loud: I AM FREE INDEED!

The next page begins your journaling of your prayer to God for day four.

Journal Your Prayer

Day 4

Today's date:_____

_____
_____
_____
_____
_____
_____
_____
_____
_____
_____
_____
_____
_____

Day 5

Fasting

Just as I mentioned earlier, that Rome was not built in a day, your discovery of your identity will take time and effort. It takes more than prayer to build a foundation for your relationship with God. Although prayer is vital in the process, fasting is also a key element in discovering your identity and building your foundation with God. There are many levels in this journey, and the first level must be built strong in order for it to last.

When I think about the story of Job, the thing I think about most is the commitment and faith he had in trusting God; despite all of his losses and his sickness, he never cursed God as his wife urged him to do in Job 2:9 (KJV): "Then said his wife unto him, Dost thou still retain thine integrity? curse God, and die." He remained steadfast and faithful through it all. The foundation of his faith, I can assure you, did not come just through prayer but also through fasting. Some things only come through prayer and fasting. At one point in the book of Matthew, Jesus casts out a demon that the disciples were unable to cast out. When they ask Jesus why they couldn't, he answers them with Matthew 17:21 (KJV): "Howbeit this kind goeth not out but by praying and fasting."

So, in order to build your foundation, begin to fast. Starting tomorrow, for the next five days . . . fast! Give up that one thing (or more) that you have grown so attached to or feel you cannot do without. By doing this, not only are you building your foundation of faith, but you're also discovering your identity and your relationship with God. He will see that you are not just talking the talk but also walking the walk and discovering who you are!

Now, when fasting, set a timetable for your start and finish. During your time of fast, commit yourself to studying, reading, or praying as well. Meditate on the words and promises of God. Spending time with God and getting to know him not only builds you up but also, believe it or not, builds your faith foundation. So, when the storms of life come your way, you will look them in the face and tell your storm that this, too, shall pass.

Remember, the storms come in all shapes and sizes. They aren't just physical, and they do not only apply to you; they can attack those that are close to you as well. Keeping the faith, fasting, and praying through the storm lets the enemy know that your foundation is not made by man's hand but is built on the Word of God!

> Fasting is to be done with the object of seeking to know God in a deeper experience (Isaiah 58:1; Zechariah 7:5). Fasting relates to a time of confession (Psalms 69:10). Fasting can be a time of seeking a deeper prayer experience and drawing near to God in prevailing prayer (Ezra 8:23; Joel 2:12). The early church often fasted in seeking God's will for leadership in the local church (Acts 13:2). When the early church wanted to know the mind of God, there was a time of praying and fasting. (Andrew Robert Fausset, M.A., D.D., "Definition for 'Fasting' Fausset's Bible Dictionary." bible-history.com/faussets; 1878.)

The next page begins your journaling of your prayer to God for day five.

Journal Your Prayer

Day 5

Today's date:_____

_____
_____
_____
_____
_____
_____
_____
_____
_____
_____
_____
_____
_____
_____

Day 6

Attacks

Your first day of fasting during this journey will prepare you for what is to come. If you have not yet experienced any strange events occurring, wait for it; the true test has just begun. You see, you are saying to the adversary that you're out on a quest seeking God, and that nothing is going to stop you from knowing God, building a foundation with him, and discovering your true identity!

I recall my first prayer quest, seeking to know God and discover my identity. I was attacked with so many obstacles, one after the other: my job gave me trouble; my health declined; and my kids, for some strange reason, started misbehaving. The attacks continued to come; it seemed like the more I fasted and prayed, the more they came. But I did not quit, I just prayed a little harder and fasted a little longer. I went from fasting during one meal a day to only eating one meal a day. I wanted the enemy to know that he would not deter me from discovering my identity and my true calling from God.

Your calling can be described as the assignment that God has ordained and placed on your life, yours alone. This special gift is why you were created, because you have purpose. But it's up to YOU! God has set you apart; remember, you are a prophet for the nations. God has BIG plans for you. "'For I know the plans I have for you,' declares the Lord, 'plans to prosper you and not to harm you, plans to give you hope and a future'" (Jeremiah 29:11, NIV).

The attacks were just a reminder that, whatever I was doing, I was making a difference and it was changing me.

Remember to stay in the race; don't throw in the towel! Keep praying, fasting, and, most of all, building your foundation, which is B.E.L.I.E.V.I.N.G.! Think of the word *believing* as an acronym: **B**eating **E**very **L**ie, **I**llusion, **E**vil-thought, **V**exed-spirit **I**nto **N**egative **G**rowth. In order for something to grow, it requires nourishing; if you don't nourish your problems by feeding them, listening to the lies, and worrying, they will surely die. When you believe, there is nothing that the enemy can do to stop you! Believing is the antidote to your problems. Stop feeding your problems and start believing your God!

The next page begins your journaling of your prayer to God for day six.

Journal Your Prayer

Day 6

Today's date:_____

Day 7

Getting Ready

Second day of your five-day fasting. I never told you it would be easy! By now, you should have a good glimpse of who you are! You see, the adversary does not like the fact that you are seeking and searching to know your God and your true identity!

Spending seven days with God—reading, praising, worshipping, meditating, and journaling your prayers—is no easy task. But it brings out the best in you, and the power of your strength and the determination that lies within you helps you to keep going.

Although you are journaling your prayers and fasting, you still must read the Word of God. The Word is our weapon! As it says in Hebrews 4:12 (KJV):

> For the word of God is quick, and powerful, and sharper than any two-edged sword, piercing even to the dividing asunder of soul and spirit, and of the joints and marrow, and is a discerner of the thoughts and intents of the heart.

When the enemy comes in like a flood, which he will, you must be ready for him. You must prepare your ammunition, the Word of God: Hebrews 4:12, Philippians 4:3, John 8:36, Jeremiah 29:11, and so on. You must keep your ammo in your soul; if you don't have the Word of God in your soul, you will fall. But even if you do fall, don't stay down, get back up. And when you have gotten back up from being talked about, lied to, abused, beaten, robbed, raped, mistreated, or hurt, you will come up with all the power you need to stand, because you are a child of the most high God, and God is a God of second chances.

Don't let the problems of life you are facing bury you; bury your problems instead. Today, speak a word of encouragement over your life; speak this prayer out loud to your problems, or to whatever situation has been haunting you with pain and misery:

Today, I release you from out of my life; you will no longer have me trapped with thoughts of doubt and disbelief. I am persuaded, with a made-up mind, that my battles do not belong to me but to my God. God has already paid the cost when he died on Calvary for my sins; the blood he shed for me has released me from all grief and pain. I will not let your fiery darts and attacks destroy me. Today, I bury you, I have erased you from my mind; you will no longer keep me tangled in the lies you replay in my mind. Today, I release you from my spirit; you are defeated and will forever be gone from my growth of spiritual development, my success in life, and my path of promises that God has for me. Today, you have lost this battle forevermore. I take back everything and reclaim the victory once again. In Jesus' name, I decree and declare that every word which has been spoken out of my mouth will go forth. *Freedom*, I welcome you into this vessel. *Peace*, you will dwell in this temple. *Joy*, you will rest upon this spirit. And *Love*, you will capture the very best in me and for others. In Jesus' name, amen.

As you discover your identity and build a closer relationship with God, please quote your favorite scriptures daily. Let it be something that consumes you. Read aloud your scriptures every morning before you start your day and every night before you go to bed. You must always be ready for whatever trap the adversary is plotting and planning for you; a soldier never goes into battle without his weapon and neither shall you!

The next page begins your journaling of your prayer to God for day seven.

Journal Your Prayer

Day 7

Today's date:_____

Day 8

Stages

New beginnings aid you in finding your true identity and building a healthier and stronger relationship with God. So far, you have been fasting for three days, along with praying, reading the Word of God, and meditating. You should start to feel or see a change emerging in you. The more you spend time with God, the more you begin to discover who you are.

At times, during my first prayer journey, I didn't think I would make it through another day. I was praying three times a day, not just speaking words that sounded good, but pouring out my feelings and heart to God, such as letting him know how I really felt about not getting the job I had wanted. I became discouraged over not getting answers to any of my prayers, which brought negative thoughts to me, until I started thinking that it was never going to come to me.

It wasn't until later that I discovered that not having the answer right away does not mean that God has forgotten you. It does not mean he doesn't care and it certainly doesn't mean he can't do it. Those doubts and that type of mindset come from the adversary. Don't get entangled by what you can see; faith comes not by things that are seen, but through believing. And, as it says in Galatians 6:9 (KJV): "And let us not be weary in well doing: for in due season we shall reap, if we faint not."

Keep pressing on and trusting God by reading the Word, praising, and praying. Patience is a virtue; it takes time to develop anything. You were not formed overnight; after you were conceived it took nine months to form you. During the course of those nine months, you began to develop in stages, and something miraculous occurs during every stage of life up until the time of birth. Although each stage of life is important, the very first stage is critical; it is at the beginning of this stage that life begins to emerge. The embryo begins to develop in the image of God—the head, arms, legs, fingers, toes, and eyes are all formed in the first stages of development. This is the foundation of your life; the abilities to think, see, hear, walk, taste, and touch are all created during this stage. As the process continues, the embryo gets bigger and stronger and becomes a fetus; then, in the final stages, the fetus becomes able to survive on its own outside of the mother's womb and is birthed through the mother's canal and called a baby.

The process we must endure in coming to God has stages as well; just like the first trimester of a baby is the most critical, so too is your first stage in developing your foundation. It must be made solid by studying and feeding on the Word of God. It's during that time that you begin to develop your spiritual insight; your eyes, ears, taste, sense of smell, walk, talk, all these will change. The things you did before, you see yourself not doing again; those bad habits seem to become less difficult to break. The more you continue to grow and study the Word of God, the more spiritual and physical changes take place.

The first level of your spiritual growth is the foundation, building a solid, firm place to stand on the Word when all hell breaks loose and you are between a rock and a hard place. The Word will bring light at the end of your tunnel. The second level of your spiritual growth is going through trials and tests, as trials only come to make you stronger. What seems impossible to man is not impossible to God. For with God, all things are possible. The second level will measure your faith, but also increase it. As you endure the tests, you also build your testimonies. These stories of your spiritual struggles will encourage others as well as yourself. The third level of your spiritual growth will be the level of all levels, the final level, your Omega, life after death, where we shall live for eternity with God.

There are stages of development from the time you are born to the time you die. Growth is not a bad thing; in fact, in order to get to your true identity, you must GROW! Think of this formula whenever you see or hear the word GROW:

God's Righteousness > Our Weakness

God's Righteousness is greater than Our Weakness. When God revealed to me this formula, he opened up my spiritual vision to see that he is bigger than our problems and our weaknesses, and when we allow him in, we enter into GROW.

The next page begins your journaling of your prayer to God for day eight.

Journal Your Prayer

Day 8

Today's date:_____

_____

_____

_____

_____

_____

_____

_____

_____

_____

_____

_____

_____

_____

_____

Day 9

Discovery

Nine straight days of praying and four days of fasting. How do you feel? Most of you, if the truth be told, will find that you are tired and becoming distracted; life is getting a little hectic, and you have lost your momentum. Stop making excuses! That's exactly what Satan wants you to feel and believe: that you can't keep up. You are built to last! And in order to discover that, you must stay on your knees. No one said building a relationship is easy; it's a process, especially when building a relationship with God.

In order to discover you, you must discover him. Only God can reveal the true identity of you. No scientist or scholar has the ability to provide that for you. They may be able to examine someone's DNA and use it to reveal their sex, eye color, race, hair color, or possible disorders, but only God can reveal to you your purpose, why you exist. Only God can show you where your strengths lie and how to fulfill the plan that he has not only ordained but anointed you to do. Yes, I said anointed; you are anointed to do certain things that no other person can do. Your task might be similar to another's task, but they will not be exactly alike, just as no two people do things entirely alike. Michael Jordan does not play ball like LeBron James. Venus Williams doesn't play tennis like her sister Serena. In the Bible, David and Saul did not serve as king in the same way; although they were both appointed and anointed by God as king, they each had a different assignment and calling on their lives. Your worship will not be like mine, but it is still pleasing to God; your duty or assignment will not be like mine, but it will be pleasing to God if it's done for his glory.

Just as the anointing is placed upon you, it can also be taken off if you become greedy in your prosperity. Know that you are not your own; as it says in 1 Corinthians 6:19 (NIV): "Do you not know that your bodies are temples of the Holy Spirit, who is in you, whom you have received from God? You are not your own." Rather, it is God that has created you out of dust; you were formed by him and the very air you breathe belongs to him.

God has given us the tools to live and to survive anything that comes before us. As you proceed through the next level of your spiritual journey, it will prepare you for battles, fiery darts, disappointments, hurt, pain, betrayal, sorrow, fear, and doubts.

Remember that tests only come to make us strong; keep praying, keep fasting, and keep journaling all of your prayers, which will turn into promises and manifest into testimonies. As a television broadcast might say during an interruption . . . THIS IS ONLY A TEST!

The next page begins your journaling of your prayer to God for day nine.

Journal Your Prayer

Day 9

Today's date:_____

Day 10

Ready Your Weapons

You have made it through the last day of your fasting and ten whole days in prayer with Abba Father. Your prayer life should be becoming comfortable, and approaching God when you are praying should now feel easier.

Your channels of prayer should now be deep and wide; you now know that God works in many ways to get his point across. You should be discovering that God has a sense of humor, too. Your conversation with God should be more personal, whether it is through speaking, singing, dancing, or journaling. You are making it your own.

It's a beautiful feeling to praise and worship God in your own way, unlike any other person, with just you and God. Once you have discovered that piece of your identity, you are well on your way. Satan's time is almost up! He can no longer use the mind games of your past; you are no longer giving him the access to enter into your mind; you are being shifted from level one to level two of your spiritual journey.

You are now beginning to operate in the Holy Spirit, leaving the things of the flesh to rot and die. Once you are under the direction of the Holy Spirit, it will lead and guide you; it will order your steps and keep you on the path of righteousness.

As you begin to operate in the spirit, rather than the flesh, you must have on the proper attire and be ready for the spiritual battles you will face. Therefore, you must be ready to put on the whole armor of God:

Finally, my brethren, be strong in the Lord, and in the power of his might. Put on the whole armor of God, that you may be able to stand against the wiles of the devil. For we wrestle not against flesh and blood, but against principalities, against powers, against the rulers of the darkness of this world, against spiritual wickedness in heavenly places. Therefore take unto you the whole armor of God, that you may be able to withstand in the evil day, and having done all, to stand. Stand therefore, having your loins girded about with truth, and having put on the breastplate of righteousness; and your feet shod with the preparation of the gospel of peace; above all, taking the shield of faith, with which you shall be able to quench all the fiery darts of the wicked one. And take the helmet of salvation, and the sword of the Spirit, which is the word of God: praying always with all prayer and supplication in the Spirit, and watching thus with all perseverance and supplication for all saints. Ephesians 6:10–18 (NKJV)

This armor will keep you and protect you from the attacks of Satan and his cronies. You will have charge over your life and be in the place of authority, where you should have been all along. The authority lies within you; you are now beginning to unleash it and operate fully in it! It's time to take your position and rule over your life; you have been in the passenger seat far too long, it's time for you to take control and get into the driver seat and drive!

The next page begins your journaling of your prayer to God for day ten.

Journal Your Prayer

Day 10

Today's date:_____

Day 11

Stormy Weather

The storm is only beginning; level two is the test of your faith. How strong is your foundation? Are you capable of standing on the Word of God? Will you fall to Satan's lies? I've been here so many times, and I must tell you that you might fall, but it's okay; the key to falling is to not stay down but instead to get back up. Remember the word GROW: in order to grow, you must learn from your mistakes; even though you know someone with the answers, God, your faith will still be tested.

Remember that trials only come to make you strong; after you have been tested, your trial becomes a testimony, as I mentioned earlier. And once you have conquered one test, you are better prepared for the next one, for each test makes you much more knowledgeable and seasoned for the trials that lie ahead.

Too often we get knocked down or caught off guard by the tests we face, thinking that we already have all the answers. You see, my brothers and sisters, when a storm arises, it never comes back the same way twice; it grows stronger and gets harder. It even comes in different shapes and sizes, and it may not be aimed directly at you, but instead those that are close to you.

That's why you should not just prepare yourself, but also be always ready: "Therefore be ye also ready: for in such an hour as ye think not the Son of man cometh" Matthew 24:44 (KJV). Be ready for whatever comes your way, having the armor of God on every time. Never take off your armor, for when you do, you are relaying to the adversary that you are letting your guard down. Remember, Satan goes around seeking whom he may devour; the minute you put your guard down, the attacks come; the minute you decide to not pray or study the Word for a day, the attacks come.

Don't be fooled, these are attacks to hurt you. But more than that, these attacks are to lure you into sin. Satan knows that, at this point, you are armed and dangerous, ready to fight off the fiery darts of trials and tribulations—but are you armed to destroy the attacks of temptations? Temptations come in many forms: fame, pride, money, cars, jewelry, sex, lust, men, women, drugs, alcohol, the list goes on; how will you cope?

Don't ever get comfortable, but be ye also ready, children of God. Our walk is never finished in this life; in fact, this is only the beginning, so we must continue to watch and pray!

The next page begins your journaling of your prayer to God for day eleven.

Journal Your Prayer

Day 11

Today's date:_____

Day 12

Things Going Wrong

In order for your faith to be at a place where you truly trust God, you will go through storms, setbacks, and pain. You do not become exempted from this; in fact, you become a target!

You are a target because you have made up your mind to only serve God, and that your past is behind you and will no longer haunt you. When you come to this point in building your relationship with God, you are discovering your identity. You are discovering what you are really made of; you are discovering your inner strength, your stamina, and the power that lies within you; you are discovering how to continue when you think you don't have enough will to fight, when you feel you are sick and tired of being sick and tired and want to quit.

Building your spiritual foundation will increase your faith despite the storms of life; cry if you have to, but continue to worship God, continue to pray! Yes, my child, pray, for it is vital in continuing to both build your relationship with God and discover your identity.

When I went through this period, everything that could go wrong, did go wrong—my kids were acting up, my job was getting overwhelming, people I thought were my friends betrayed and left me, some family members became distant and turned their backs on me. The only person you can call on in such times is our God.

Throughout this battle, some days I just wanted to quit and be mad at the world. But my communication with God through praying, journaling, and worshipping is what kept me going. It wasn't through me calling my best friend or talking to my mom, it was through my prayer time with God that I found my willpower to continue, my motivation, my encouragement. God gave me the answer I needed to continue through his words: "Put not your trust in princes, nor in the son of man, in whom there is no help" Psalm 146:3 (KJV). And, "It is better to trust in the Lord than to put confidence in man. It is better to trust in the Lord than to put confidence in princes" Psalm 118:8–9 (KJV).

When all else fails, put your trust in God, for God never fails!

The next page begins your journaling of your prayer to God for day twelve.

Journal Your Prayer

Day 12

Today's date:_____

Day 13

Why

It takes time to build your faith and time to build the relationship you want with God. As a matter of fact, you should start to consider: *why* do you want to build your faith and relationship with God?

In network marketing, they say, you must have a strong *why* to stay in the industry, because you are going to face a lot of disappointment and feel discouragement over even staying in the game. Having that strong *why* is what will keep you grounded and refusing to give up. Some of your *why*s could be: wanting to provide the finer things for your children, wanting a better life for yourself, not wanting to work for other people, or wanting to be your own boss and own your own business. These are good reasons, but they are not always enough. Once something goes wrong enough or you become too tired of being rejected, you want to quit; even though you remember your *why*, you still want to bail out.

The reason why I know this is true is because this was my story. A few years back, I joined the world of network marketing and, eventually, bailed out after getting a few too many rejections and not getting enough support. I, too, thought I had a strong *why*, but it wasn't enough. This is how we feel sometimes when we are building our faith and putting our trust in God. We start out determined that nothing is going to interfere in our relationship with God; but the minute storms, pain (such as the death of loved ones), or setbacks come our way, we second-guess and forget our *why*. We pray and pray; yet, the more we pray, the harder it gets, so why bother?

This is what Satan wants you to think; if he can secure those doubts in your mind, voila! He's caught you! Once he has you caught, he will continue to feed you with doubt, until sooner or later you just give up and quit. Never give up on yourself! In order to change, you must grow, and in order to grow, you must change; they go hand in hand. Remember Hebrews 11:1 (KJV): "Now faith is the substance of things hoped for, the evidence of things not seen." Just because you cannot see it does not mean it doesn't exist. God is alive in you, he operates in you, and he will guide you if you give him the opportunity.

Building your faith and your relationship with God is a lengthy process; it takes gradual steps to discover God the Father and figure out who you are. But you have begun these steps, from when you started your first day of reading this book and thus made that commitment with God. Continue to take steps along this journey of praying, reading the Word, worshipping, fasting, believing, and journaling!

Write down on the next page your *why*, reminding yourself and God why you are seeking to discover your true identity and build a stronger relationship with him.

The next page begins your journaling of your prayer to God for day thirteen.

Journal Your Prayer

Day 13

Today's date:_____

_____

_____

_____

_____

_____

_____

_____

_____

_____

_____

_____

_____

_____

Day 14

Your Result

Today, if you are reading this page, you have been journaling for thirteen days straight. You have been consistent. This is key, people of God; we must be consistent in our praying, worshipping, fasting, journaling, and praising! We must remain consistent in finding our true identity and our relationship with God.

This is the hardest part in building a relationship, but it is the key to your discovery: your change. Every day, when you go for a walk or exercise at the gym, you don't see change right away; but through consistency, in about four to six weeks, you see a change. If you continue, ultimately, you get to the place you want to be. My question to you is: what result do you want to reach with God?

I asked you in day thirteen of your journaling to write down your *why*; now I am asking you today to write down the result you want in your relationship with God. Do you want to have a casual relationship, an intimate relationship, or an everlasting relationship with God? Take some time to ponder on this, for with each successive level of your relationship comes different tests and trials of your faith; the deeper you want to go with God, the harder it will become.

When you begin to write down your thoughts, consider Habakkuk 2:2b (ESV): "Write the vision; make it plain on tablets, so he may run who reads it." Try to make it clear what your goal is so you will know how to act. Then, every day, take action to work toward your end result, so that you reach what you want it to be, what you wrote down. Remember, if you want that everlasting relationship, then you will have to be consistent—there's that word again—for the rest of your days, for everlasting has no end time; God's love is everlasting, never ending.

When I think about my relationship with God and where I want my end result to be, I begin to think on all of the things God has done for me and all of the situations he has brought me out of; his word is forever faithful and his promises are real.

It's just an amazing feeling to know that, no matter what you pick your relationship to be with him, his love for you is everlasting!

The next page begins your journaling of your prayer to God for day fourteen.

Journal Your Prayer

Day 14

Today's date:_____

_____
_____
_____
_____
_____
_____
_____
_____
_____
_____
_____
_____
_____
_____

Day 15

Halfway There

You are halfway there in your thirty days of journaling your prayers, discovering your identity, and getting a closer relationship with God. Today, I want you to reflect over the last fourteen days and note a change that has occurred—because a change did happen. You have been consistent in your praying, fasting, and studying of the Word. Therefore, I know without a shadow of a doubt that something has happened. Jot it down and recall all that happened during this life-changing event. This is truly an event that is going to change your life; you cannot be the same once you have an encounter with God.

How has it been so far for you? Is it hard? Do you feel like giving up? Do you pray three times a day? What are your conversations like with God? Are they more personal, or still traditional? Are you hearing from God? Where is your faith level?

My most important question to you is: are you still standing? You have made it halfway, if you are reading these pages; you have prayed for fifteen of your thirty days of journaling your prayers, you've studied the Word of God every day, and you are changing. Although we can't stop bad things from happening, we have been building our faith and standing on the Word of God. As it says in Isaiah 54:17 (KJV):

> No weapon that is formed against thee shall prosper; and every tongue that shall rise against thee in judgment thou shalt condemn. This is the heritage of the servants of the Lord, and their righteousness is of me, saith the Lord.

Just the thought that no weapons formed against me shall prosper has me dancing and shouting and giving God all the praise.

You are protected from the time you wake up every morning until the time you lay your head down to sleep every night. God has you shielded by the Blood of Jesus. The God you serve is keeping you and sheltering you; when life seems as if it is going to cave in on you, just stand on the Word. God's Word is life, it is power, and it is your strength that you will need when faced with all types of adversity.

The Word of God is the antidote to your problems. Remember that weapons will form, but they will not prosper; this is a sure guarantee from God the Father, who sent his only Son Jesus Christ. When I looked up the word guarantee, Webster defines it as the following:

> Guarantee—A promise on assurance, especially one in writing, that something is of specified quality, content, benefit, etc., or that it will perform satisfactorily for a given length of time; a money-back guarantee.

God is the Guarantor—one who grants it—if he says it, it's a guarantee that it will happen!

The next page begins your journaling of your prayer to God for day fifteen.

Journal Your Prayer

Day 15

Today's date:_____

Day 16

I Am

Now that you have surpassed the halfway point, you would normally think that things would get easier; well, I hate to burst your bubble, but this is the time when things continue to build against you. That's right, things build against you; why, you ask? Because you are discovering your true identity. You are talking to your Father and building that relationship with him.

You are finding out that, during the storms, you can stand on the rock of God's faithfulness, which is higher than yourself. You are finding out that "if God is for us, who can be against us?" (Romans 8:31b, NIV). You are finding out that, if you stand on God's Word, it builds the faith that is within you; it's building you up to be able to say that the God you serve is able in all things.

God has also revealed in you that he has a plan for you; if he has not already revealed it, it will come! Just keep seeking him. The plan that God has for you will bless you; and it will not only bless you, but God will use it to bless everything that is around you. God's blessing overflows . . . it reaches the highest mountains and flows to the lowest valley. God's blessing, just like the blood of his Son, will give you the strength you need, the power to stand.

So, what does Satan do when his back is against the wall? He throws surprise attacks! Yes, these attacks will blindside you; you won't see them coming, so remember to keep the armor of God on daily to help protect you from the surprise attacks! Satan's attacks are a testing of your faith. You've heard the saying: actions speak louder than words. You know that Satan is the father of lies, and he knows that the best tactic he has is to put doubt in you. Remember, don't take the bait.

When surprises come, stay the course and speak a word over yourself; begin to speak your true identity, which is:

I AM a Child of God.

I AM able to do all things except fail.

I AM victorious.

I AM powerful.

I AM rich.

I AM healed.

I AM _____.

Fill in your I AM and speak to whatever attack that comes; say I AM an overcomer, which mean I will overcome.

Whatever the current situation that is being thrown at you, say to it:

I AM what God say I AM and shall become who God say I will be!

The next page begins your journaling of your prayer to God for day sixteen.

> # Journal Your Prayer

Day 16

Today's date:_____

Day 17

No Doubt

Now, today I will ask: where are you on your level of faith? How has this journey helped you in making decisions and giving God control over the circumstances you are faced with? We have the tendency to think that God needs our assistance, but he already has help; he is the Trinity. God is the Father, Son, and Holy Spirit; if he needed more, he would have said so.

Your assistance will only be an interference, you will only get in the way of what God is trying to do and teach you. I know what you are saying: when will it happen? Did I do something to hinder God from answering me? The answer to these most-asked questions are: soon, and no. It will happen soon; in fact, when you have built your faith to a certain level, you will not ask the question when, but you will instead begin to thank God, because you will know it's a guarantee that it will happen.

The "No" is that God will never withhold anything good from his faithful people, just as it says in Psalm 84:11 (ASV): "For Jehovah God is a sun and shield: Jehovah will give grace and glory; No good thing will he withhold from them that walk uprightly." The key thought to keep in your spirit is that nothing you can do can stop God from loving you. God loves us unconditionally, so don't believe the lies that Satan will say to you. Don't allow doubt to get into your mind. No doubt, keep Satan out! Let this be your chant, say it out loud: NO DOUBT, KEEP SATAN OUT!

Your level of faith grows at the level of your relationship with God. If you want that certainty—no doubt, worries, or fear—it will require that you continue to build, much harder than you already are. If you are praying, fasting, worshipping, and reading the

Word, go deeper and begin to speak it not only to yourself, but also to your spouse, children, friends, family, and coworkers.

The more you speak on the goodness of God and what he can do, the more you will build your faith and the more you will be able to motivate others, just as the Father motivates you through his words. Encouraging yourself is the key to building a solid faith!

The next page begins your journaling of your prayer to God for day seventeen.

Journal Your Prayer

Day 17

Today's date:_____

Day 18

In Your DNA

This is a great vantage point to speak on your identity; who are you? You have not only been praying, fasting, reading, and worshipping, but you have also been studying, observing, and seeing a change in yourself. After all, you have been spending a lot of time with God. For seventeen consecutive days you have been communicating with God. So, I ask you, who are you? Has God revealed to you your DNA? What are you made of? Do you even have a clue as to how powerful you are?

Let me give you the definition of DNA and why it is important. DNA, also known as Deoxyribonucleic acid, is a nucleic acid that contains the genetic instructions used in the development and functioning of all living organisms. DNA is what tells the cells how they are to function; without DNA, there would be no cell division and therefore no growth.

The importance of DNA is that it is the universal blueprint of life on Earth. DNA determines what people look like and how their bodies will function.

Now let's take a look at this spiritually. We are made up of God's DNA: "So God created mankind in his own image, in the image of God he created them; male and female he created them" (Genesis 1:27, NIV). We look like God, so why is it that we don't walk like God, talk like God, or even think like God? Is it because we are afraid that we can't be like God?

We should not be afraid, for we can and will do great things. John 14:12 (KJV) tells us: "Verily, verily, I say unto you, He that believeth on me, the works that I do shall he do also; and greater works than these shall he do; because I go unto my Father." If God's Word says that we shall do greater, then why are you struggling with your identity when it comes to doing the unthinkable, the incredible? You can do it all; you not only have the DNA that makes you who you are, but you also have the intercessor, Jesus, who goes to the Father. Just like the little engine that could, you can do it if you think you can. You have all the substance you need on the inside of you; it's who you are, it's in your DNA!

Finding your inner strength will ignite the flames in you, but believing will grant you access to all of the possibilities that you can ever ask or think. As you read the pages of this book, remember: I would never have imagined that I would be the author of a book speaking to so many about the goodness of God; all I knew was that I had more to give, I had purpose in this life here on earth, and I wanted to explore all of it. This is just the beginning of what my future holds. It's never too late, so don't let anything stop you from discovering your purpose or the reason why you were placed here on this earth.

The next page begins your journaling of your prayer to God for day eighteen.

Journal Your Prayer

Day 18

Today's date:_____

_____
_____
_____
_____
_____
_____
_____
_____
_____
_____
_____
_____
_____
_____

Day 19

The Power of Your Words

Be careful what you say and the words that come out of your mouth. "The tongue has the power of life and death, and those who love it will eat its fruit" (Proverbs 18:21, NIV). Just today, I had a surprise attack. Remember how, earlier in this book, I spoke of those attacks that catch you by surprise, and what your response should be as a child of God? Well, it happened to me. I went to the doctor's office today for a preventive screening, only to discover that my blood pressure level was through the roof, very high. The first reading was 135/88, and the nurse asked if I normally have high blood pressure. I replied that I didn't, so she said that she would come back and take it again in a few minutes.

So at that point, I was supposed to go into an uproar of worrying over what was going on with me, thinking, "I am doing everything right, I just don't understand." Instead, I remained calm and began to look on my phone so the enemy would not distract me by putting the spirit of worry in me. After about three minutes passed, the nurse came back and took the reading again; but this time it was even higher—yes, that's right, I said higher, the result was 153/115! So at this point, Satan wanted me to lose it, but I still remained calm and said out loud Isaiah 53:5 (KJV): "But he was wounded for our transgressions, he was bruised for our iniquities: the chastisement of our peace was upon him; and with his stripes we are healed."

I declared healing over my body, for my blood pressure to go back to normal. Instead of getting frantic and upset, I remained calm. After my visit I did not worry. I began to pray with a prayer partner and gave God praise, asking him to restore my blood pressure back to a level where it wouldn't cause any damage to my health.

I was not and am not ignoring the fact that high blood pressure can be deadly and that I should take it seriously; oh, but I do. But one thing I recalled from my visit with my doctor stuck with me. She first asked me if I was okay, if I knew what was going on, as she was just as surprised as I was. Then she asked, "Do either of your parents have high blood pressure?" I replied that yes, they both do.

What she said after that really struck me: "Oh, well, it's genetic, it's your genes, you can't change the family you were born into or the genes they carry." I immediately connected what she said with being part of God's family. We cannot escape it, it's genetic; we are children of God. We are connected to his genes, we are a royal priesthood, we have been bought with a price. God's love for us will never die. The makeup of our genes is that of God. I got excited when I heard that and declared my healing.

The words I spoke over myself were: I am connected to God, I have his genes, it's unchangeable and untransferable; therefore, I am healed! I share this story to encourage you to hold on, and to not give up! God is a healer and deliverer from all sickness and pain. If you are on medication, confess that you are healed each day when you take your medication. Your words are powerful and will help bring about a change when you believe what you are speaking. People of God, 1 Peter 2:9 (KJV) says it best: "But ye are a chosen generation, a royal priesthood, an holy nation, a peculiar people; that ye should shew forth the praises of him who hath called you out of darkness into his marvellous light." Remember the key words in this scripture: *chosen generation*, *royal priesthood*, *an holy nation*, and *a peculiar people*. Therefore, you should not allow worrying, stress, or anxiety to come upon you, because God has called you out of darkness. If you do worry, you will develop the mindset of thinking that you will not be healed. Instead, believe that you have control over your life and the condition in how you choose to live it.

The next week, when I went to visit my primary doctor, the reading of my blood pressure was normal; it was 134/83. To God be the glory! I stood on the word of Isaiah 53:5 and believed . . . NO DOUBT, KEEP SATAN OUT!

The next page begins your journaling of your prayer to God for day nineteen.

Journal Your Prayer

Day 19

Today's date:_____

Day 20

Fret Not

Fret not! As John 16:33 (KJV) says: "These things I have spoken unto you, that in me ye might have peace. In the world ye shall have tribulation: but be of good cheer; I have overcome the world." Today you have just entered into twenty days of being in constant communication with God. Now, when I say constant, I don't mean that before this you didn't spend time with God. We do communicate with God frequently; but, if you are honest with yourself, you may find you have never before taken the time to discover all there is to know about yourself and your connection with God.

You don't have to wait until the storms come to spend more time than usual with God. Remember that the Father knows; there are no surprises for him. Just in spending an hour or two with him each day, you will discover something amazing about God and, most importantly, about yourself.

Twenty days is significant; the biblical meaning of the number twenty is redemption, being redeemed and forgiven of all of your sins, errors, or causes of destruction. Today, as you are recording your prayer on your journal page, I want you to write down what you have discovered thus far on your journey to find your identity and deepen your relationship with God. Be honest with yourself; express to God your true thoughts and feelings; be transparent.

Express the things you are still waiting on God to deliver and how you feel about them. Share with God what you have learned so far from praying to him on a more consistent basis. Consider the various techniques you have used to accomplish your journey. Share what you still need to work on, your shortcomings and the struggles you are having in believing. Some of you were probably weary well before the twenty day mark, but it's okay. Remember, we all have shortcomings, but it is how you bounce back that matters. If you keep on praying, fasting, reading the Word, and praising God in the midst of your situation, God will bless you and set you free from the captive mindset you have, that not everything is going to work out the way you want it to. That's true, but things will always work out the way God intended for them to. We don't have the answers to all of life's circumstances, but we know who does. The question you need to ask yourself is: do I believe? Do I believe that my God is bigger than my problems? Situations? Circumstances? Conditions? Pain? Hurt? Guilt? Sin? When you draw your own conclusion that he will, leave it there and wait.

In the midst of your waiting, you will not only discover your identity, you will also become an expert. Yes, you will become the expert in being able to wait patiently. This sounds easy, but it is one of the hardest things to do. With the world now bringing everything on with speed, and with our ability to get almost everything we need in just a click of a button, the waiting process can seem unnecessary. But God wants you to wait and, in your waiting, become the expert in building your faith and your strength.

The next page begins your journaling of your prayer to God for day twenty.

Journal Your Prayer

Day 20

Today's date:_____

Day 21

Forming a Habit

Dr. Maxwell Maltz, in his book *Psycho-Cybernetics*, discussed how it takes a minimum of twenty-one days to form a new habit. Today is day twenty-one of your journaling, reading, praying, fasting, and worshipping unto the Lord our God. What has become your new habit? Do you find your praying to God much easier now? Have you found that you now have your own words to say, instead of just saying something you have memorized from childhood?

Forming a habit requires consistency, obedience, and, of course, sacrifice. You made the commitment to yourself to be consistent in praying, worshipping, fasting, and journaling for these thirty days. You sacrificed sleep; food; addictions to social media, TV shows, etc.; and routine habits to spend time with God during this process. And finally, you became obedient by not only reading the pages in this book but also recording your prayers.

Habits form change. Let me repeat that again, habits form change. Now that you have been doing this type of communicating with God, you have changed your ways. The way you communicate with God will change, the way you pray, talk, and listen to God. You will be more inclined to hear his voice. You have changed your spiritual prayer life. The more you do it, the better you will become at it. This method not only applies to your spiritual life, but to anything you do in life; you learn and become better through repetition. But what you don't know is that God doesn't want you to merely become better, because he already knows that you are great! He that is great is within us, and he helps us to be greater still. As 1 John 4:4 (KJV) tells us: "Ye are of God, little children, and have overcome them; because greater is he that is in you, than he that is in the world."

You are great at what you do if you believe it. God knows that you are; you don't have to convince him, you have to convince yourself. You don't have to have a prayer life with big words that you might not understand to be great at praying; that doesn't mean or say anything to God. Impress God instead by giving what's real and hidden down deep on the inside of you. Give him your heart and your commitment. Don't wait until something occurs before you want to spend more time talking to God on how to fix it. Instead, do it now, create and sustain the new habit and talk real talk to God every day.

Habits form change. Start your new habit in developing your relationship with God to the next level and see a change!

The next page begins your journaling of your prayer to God for day twenty-one.

Journal Your Prayer

Day 21

Today's date:_____

_____
_____
_____
_____
_____
_____
_____
_____
_____
_____
_____
_____
_____

Day 22

Day of Reflection

What has happened thus far? Go back in your prayer journal and reread the pages from day one to day twenty-one. Do you recall anything drastic that took place? Do you have testimonies on how trials and tribulations were handled? How has your communication with God been? Have you heard from him? If so, what was your experience? Did you recall it down on paper?

Reflecting back is not always a bad thing. People sometimes say to never look back on your past, but my philosophy is, if I don't look back on it, how will I know if I have grown? I am not reliving my past, I'm simply recalling and seeing the changes or transitions that have inspired me. I look for the point at which I decided that I wanted a clearer understanding of God, that changed me so that I am now serving and making true connections with him. I don't want to live off of others' testimony; I want to start creating my own testimony that can get me through some of my moments of uncertainty.

Let's take a moment right now to reflect. Take time here to recall your past, going from where you were five years ago to where you are right now, for the next two minutes.

God has not only kept you from death and the grave, he has also kept you from dangers unseen. During your reflection, you went through the good times, the bad times, and the times you didn't think you were going to make it. But looking back taught you that you have willpower that lies within you, willpower that is connected to God. You discovered not only your true identity, but also your worth. With God, it goes without question that he values you! Your price tag is far greater than any type of money, than silver or gold, for it was paid by the life of his only begotten Son so that you might have a full and wholesome life.

God wants you to live an abundant life without lacking anything! The enemy, however, comes to destroy that abundance. As John 10:10 (KJV) says: "The thief cometh not, but for to steal, and to kill, and to destroy: I am come that they might have life, and that they might have it more abundantly."

I would like for you to let your prayer journal today be focused on how much you have grown over the course of twenty-one days and how much you have changed, despite the odds that were thrown against you. Those odds may have been the hurt that you encountered from family and friends, the lies and negativity that you received at work, the bad doctor's report, the negative report of your children's progress, the hard decision about your bills and if you might be foreclosing on your home, the eviction notice on your apartment door, or the repossession of your car, but whatever they were, you have succeeded and grown.

The simple fact is that, underneath all of that, you still have praise on the inside and a pep in your step, with both hands lifted up; it tells the enemy that he has lost the battle. The victory belongs to you! Your name spells VICTORY! You have conquered all of the weight that was burying you and was trying to take you out! You endured hardship, but you triumphed, for we know that it's not over until God says it's over!

The next page begins your journaling of your prayer to God for day twenty-two.

Journal Your Prayer

Day 22

Today's date:_____

Day 23

What's Your ID?

Seven more days until you have reached the thirtieth day of journaling prayers, worshipping, fasting, and praising God on this journey to discovery! The number seven represents completion in the biblical meaning. So today, my question to you is: What's your ID? Were you able to discover who you are? I know you know whose you are, but do you know your ID?

The person that God has called you to be is a person that has a purpose to be fulfilled on this earthly realm. You are a person of greatness, for, as it says in 1 Corinthians 6:20 (KJV), you have been bought with a price: "For ye are bought with a price: therefore glorify God in your body, and in your spirit, which are God's." And, being in the image of God, your identity is unique; you can do anything you set your mind to do. You can reach any goal you set out to do. You have limitless boundaries; you can go anywhere.

You have the authority, dominion, and power. Don't let the tactics of Satan stop you from pursuing your dreams. You can do and be anything you want to do or be. We are not like any other living creature; we have the ability to conquer whatever quest is set before us. God has given us the capability to achieve whatever we set our minds to do. Now, let me go back and ask you this question: After communicating with God for the last twenty-three days, do you still think the same way that you did before you started this journey? Has your belief level gone up, or are you still bound to only the things you can see and gain control of?

For me, during my first journey, this experience changed my thought process to the point where I no longer get anxious when things fall apart. Instead, I remain calm, think the problem out, and then pray. By doing thus, I not only alleviate stress out of my life, which can lead to hypertension and other symptoms, I also no longer feel myself becoming frustrated. My most important discovery, though, was how my personal relationship with God started blossoming; my prayers were more of a dialogue and my hearing and vision of God's words and deeds became clearer. I found myself wanting to know more of God. During that first journey, it seemed as if he never ceased to amaze me; every day, not only did I discover something miraculous about God, but I also discovered my capabilities and what I was really made of. Ford proclaims in its car and truck commercials that its vehicles are "built to last" and "built Ford tough." Well, my brothers and sisters, we are also built to last and built tough.

In our identity, we are flexible; this might seem to be an unusual word to use, but consider: being flexible means that sometimes you will bend, but you will always bounce back up. It doesn't matter which way we are stretched, we don't break, we only bend. The flexibility tells you that you can handle whatever situation comes your way, because you will become flexible about the problem and be able to deal with it!

As you discover your identity, your faith level increases; however, when your faith grows, so do all the tests of Satan. But what you will begin to realize is that the more time you spend in getting to know God, the more you will be able to identify who you are, because your identity is what you have been reading all through these pages: the three-letter word, God.

Your identity is the identity of God; you were made in his image and have taken on the authority and power that was sent to you through the Holy Comforter. When I discovered this, I knew that, from that point on, Satan wouldn't stand a chance. You see, my mindset had changed, therefore I changed the way I viewed everything! I became less doubtful and more confident that I could do the unthinkable.

My mind was expanding, I was changing, the vision seem brighter, and my future was hopeful. All of this happened once I made up in my mind: God, this is it! I am tired of being sick and tired. I want to get to know my identity and purpose and not be afraid to do what you have called me to do. Having faith is great, but we must also do as God has called us, because faith without works is dead:

> What doth it profit, my brethren, though a man say he hath faith, and have not works? can faith save him? If a brother or sister be naked, and destitute of daily food, and one of you say unto them, Depart in peace, be ye warmed and filled; notwithstanding ye give them not those things which are needful to the body; what doth it profit? Even so faith, if it hath not works, is dead, being alone. James 2:14–17 (KJV)

Begin to operate in your faith by putting in the work; the more you pray, fast, worship, and read the Word of God, the more your faith will increase. Remember, there can be no increase without putting in effort. Who are you? Consider this for your prayer today.

The next page begins your journaling of your prayer to God for day twenty-three.

Journal Your Prayer

Day 23

Today's date:_____

Day 24

Trust

How do we build trust? Some would say by spending time with the person. How do you build a relationship? Again, by spending time with the person. How do you continue to trust? By spending time with and getting to know the person. I just asked three similar but different questions, but the result from each of the questions is the same, and the one key word is *time*.

Time is valuable and can never be regained once it's gone. You will never be able to get your seconds, minutes, or hours back; once the clock strikes, that's it, we can only move on to the next twenty-four hours to try again at the start of a new day. How you spend your time is personal, but I hope that you are making every minute count.

Relationships can only be formed by spending time with the person. Studies have shown that the more you are around a person, the more you begin to pick up habits from them, whether negative or positive. This holds true for God as well. The more you communicate with God, the more you take on his characteristics, and what better characteristics could you want to duplicate than those of God? Remember, God only shows you more if you ask for more. Trust does not only come from seeing; one must also do in order to believe, and once you have done it, you have more confidence and reassurance that you can continue to do it.

The type of trust we all want does not come in an instant package. This trust takes time and development. You have to believe what you can't see, and that's one of the hardest things to do, because our material minds have trouble with expanding and reaching into the spiritual mindset. We must build our spiritual mindset through our relationship with God. Proverbs 3:5–6 (KJV) tells us: "Trust in the Lord with all thine heart; and lean not to thine own understanding. In all thy ways acknowledge him, and he shall direct thy paths." Many of us know this scripture word for word. If you haven't discovered it yet, you must realize, speaking these words has no effect on you unless you believe what you are saying!

For as long as you trust in God and operate in obedience to his word, God will direct you along the path that he will appoint you to take. Which will you choose, Trust or Decision? Ponder on the words and then the author behind the words: Trust is God and Decision is You! Don't keep making decisions that will have you living with consequences that you could have prevented if you had chosen Trust! Make the statement and work on trusting God, not just in some things, but in everything and every area of your life.

The next page begins your journaling of your prayer to God for day twenty-four.

Journal Your Prayer

Day 24

Today's date:_____

_____
_____
_____
_____
_____
_____
_____
_____
_____
_____
_____
_____
_____
_____

Day 25

Opportunity

Let the countdown begin: 5, 4, 3, 2, 1 . . . . Today is day twenty-five, only five days left in your journey. Today we will begin our second and last fast for this journey. When you start your fast, try to choose for your fast something that you know you battle with, are addicted to, or that takes a lot of your time. Let this last fast show Satan that you are all the way in! You are going hard and will finish strong. Keep in your heart this saying: "For the race is not given to the swift nor the battle to the strong, but to the one who endures to the end."

What pleases God is not your quickness or how strong you are in your physical being; what pleases God is your mindset, your thoughts and beliefs, and your knowledge that you will win and you will not be defeated, ever! Fasting does not only show God your commitment to wanting to get a closer relationship with him or your willingness to sacrifice what matters to you. It also shows your ability to resist those things that you thought you needed or couldn't do without. By fasting, you are resisting and giving up those temptations. You already have the willpower in you to resist, for it's all about the choices you make every day. Who will you choose? What choices will you make after discovering your identity and the God you serve?

After this journey—and I am saying this with confidence—you will not be the same. You have already discovered both where your strength lies and the power behind faith! Faith expands your vision; it gives you a broader perspective and outlook on things. You cannot possibly see things as you did prior to achieving a deeper relationship. Positive people encourage you to do, act, and think in such a way that, when you are at your lowest, you will know which steps to take and which moves to make. And God is surely the most positive person of all!

God is your encourager; he gives you the motivation, willpower, and drive to be like him. Once you get on board with God, you have joined with the Father of Opportunity. People often call America the Land of Opportunity, but God is the Father of Opportunity, for he will allow you the opportunity to succeed, to achieve your dreams, and to become the very thing you aspire to be. The only thing that is required is your yes. Now, keep in mind that your yes can cost you everything. Are you willing to say yes? You will be releasing the things that seem to hinder you and picking up the things that will prosper you . . . because anything that is associated with God will prosper! Finish these thirty days strong, with fasting, praying, and worshipping; let God hear your yes—not from your lips, because that's easy to do, but from your actions. Let's go!

The next page begins your journaling of your prayer to God for day twenty-five.

Journal Your Prayer

Day 25

Today's date:_____

Day 26

Plans

You have just entered into day two of your fast and day twenty-six of journaling your prayers, finding your true identity, and building your relationship with God. What have you devoted yourself to fasting from in these last five days of your journey? How will you fill that void? What has this experience been like for you? Do you feel that you have grown closer to God? Do you hear the voice of God? Why all the questions, is what you are probably thinking; but just imagine that God is asking you these questions—what would your response be?

God wants to hear how you feel; yes, he knows, but you expressing yourself to him is what he is seeking. He wants an intimate relationship with you, and, in order for it to happen, he needs your cooperation. To cooperate, especially in a relationship, requires two; as Amos 3:3 (KJV) asks us, "Can two walk together, except they be agreed?"

Walking with God requires that you agree to his commands and the plans he has for you. Remember, "the steps of a good man are ordered by the Lord: and he delighteth in his way" (Psalm 37:23, KJV). God has his plans for your life, ready on a blueprint. He has it designed, going from the time you were conceived in your mother's womb until the day you take your final breath.

I had never thought about it this way until he revealed it to me as he was using my mind and hand to write the pages of this book. Your life is a blueprint to God. He has your plan already mapped out; now it's time for you to look at it, study it, and follow it so you can build! Some of you may be wondering or asking: how do you stay on the path and with the plans that God has for you? Let me first start off by saying and speaking from experience: it is never easy. In fact, it's one of the hardest thing you will do. Staying on the path that God has for you requires discipline and obedience. It requires your will being surrendered to God's will. Remember Jesus' words in Luke 22:42 (ISV): "Father, if you are willing, take this cup away from me. Yet not my will but yours be done."

Don't allow yourself to be tricked by Satan! He will try to get you to think that, once you have fallen short, you can never get back on the path or with the plans that God has for you, but that is a bald-faced lie! God will never give up on his plans for you; what God has for you, remains for you. Remember, God is the God of a second chance!

The next page begins your journaling of your prayer to God for day twenty-six.

Journal Your Prayer

Day 26

Today's date:_____

_____
_____
_____
_____
_____
_____
_____
_____
_____
_____
_____
_____
_____
_____

Day 27

The Message

How has your prayer life been thus far, now that you have been journaling consistently for twenty-six days? What is your communication like now? Do you hear God speaking more clearly? As you have been journaling, praying, and fasting, what has changed for you? Take a moment to ponder before really answering. You have three days remaining in your journey and three days left of fasting. Now that you are so close to the end, what has changed in your spiritual walk, compared to when you started? How have you been dealing with attacks? Do you find yourself feeling less stress and trusting the Word of God more?

Prayer is powerful because it is the way we communicate with God and get to know him better. God can also send us messages in unusual ways and through unexpected people. Just the other day I was speaking to one of my friends; during our conversation, he said such a profound statement that I told him I was going to use it in my book, with his permission. As this statement left his mouth and hit my ears, I felt it in my spirit and I knew it was a message for me from God. The words that hit my ears were: "You don't have to chase nothing that the Lord has for you." So, my brothers and sisters, I am speaking to you and conveying this message to you. You don't have to chase anything that the Lord has for you. What God has for you is designed just for you. It's not intended for your spouse, daughter, son, brother, sister, mother, father, friend, or coworker. It's for you, yes, you!

God has a plan for all of us; we don't have to envy others or have malice in our hearts. God created us to be unique; each of us has a different path and purpose from God to fulfill as we spend our days here on earth. As I stated earlier in this book, I discovered my gift was the call of intercession, to be one who interceded on behalf of others. Yours could be singing, dancing, preaching, or teaching, to name a few; but whatever it is, God has already placed it in you. It's up to you to discover it and proceed.

As an intercessor, I want to pray this prayer on behalf of my brothers and sisters who are reading the words on this page:

Our Father, who art in heaven, hallowed be thy name, thy kingdom come, thy will be done, on earth as it is in heaven. Give us this day our daily bread; and forgive us our trespasses, as we forgive those who trespass against us; and lead us not into temptation, but deliver us from evil. For thine is the kingdom, and the power, and the glory, forever and ever.

Father God, I come before you on behalf of my brothers and sisters who are reading the words of this prayer. I ask that you enter into their hearts and minds and reveal to them the plans you have already ordained for their lives. I pray that you begin the shifting in their minds which will allow them to think as you think. I pray that they will have the assurance and confidence to not be afraid once you convey their gifts and your plans for them, but instead be filled with the power of your might to do what you have called them to do. I pray they will ignite their flames and begin to take flight on the assignments they will discover from the Word of God. Let this prayer be the beginning of them finding their way to the blueprint you have placed in their hearts. "And we know that all things work together for good to them that love God, to them who are the called according to his purpose" (Romans 8:28, KJV). Amen.

The next page begins your journaling of your prayer to God for day twenty-seven.

Journal Your Prayer

Day 27

Today's date:_____

Day 28

Perfect Timing

"I am who God says I am, I can do what He says I can do. I can have what He says I can have. If He said it, it will surely come to pass!" (T.D. Jakes, Twitter post, September 4, 2014, 6:50 a.m., @BishopJakes)

I am quite sure that this affirmation from Bishop T.D. Jakes was his motivation and kept him going when he was faced with adversity in his life. What is your motivation? What do you say or do when the odds are against you and your back is against the wall, when no one can help you or you have no one to turn to? When you feel that you are all alone, what do you do?

Over the past twenty-seven days I know you have discovered the Man who has all of the plans, who knows all of your needs before you speak a word or even think of them! (Imagine if you could know what a person is saying before the words come out of their mouth!) I know that, during this journey, you have developed and found what you are made of, what genes and DNA are in your body. I know that you have had some attacks, some which caught you by surprise, but that you are still standing. I know that you wanted to quit because you didn't see any results and felt like it wasn't working, but that you kept on journaling, reading, fasting, and praying.

The reason I know that these things happened is because I have been there, right in the place where you are now. I thought that God did not hear my prayers because I was not living my life like I should have been, was not living up to the level where a Christian was supposed to be. I felt that, as a child of God, I was supposed to act and be a certain way. Talk about peer pressure! But God showed me that his ways are not like our ways, neither are his thoughts like our thoughts. I did not need to hold to some human standard, I only had to follow God's will. I also found that Jesus hears all of my prayers and he intercedes for me with his father God.

Romans 8:34 (NIV) tells us: "Who then is the one that condemns? No one. Christ Jesus who died—more than that, who was raised to life—is at the right hand of God and is also interceding for us." Don't quit, for God will deliver; he may not come when you want him to, but he is always on time. God's timing is perfect, he has a set time for every circumstance, all he is asking of you is to hold on. So even after you complete this journey of journaling for thirty days, position yourself to receive your directive from God. He has all of the answers to those questions, problems, and situations that trouble your wellbeing. For the Father knows, and who can stop someone who knows it all? No one.

The next page begins your journaling of your prayer to God for day twenty-eight.

Journal Your Prayer

Day 28

Today's date:_____

_____
_____
_____
_____
_____
_____
_____
_____
_____
_____
_____
_____
_____

Day 29

Sharing the Journey

"And hath made of one blood all nations of men for to dwell on all the face of the earth, and hath determined the times before appointed, and the bounds of their habitation" (Acts 17:26, KJV).

What a mighty God we serve. Although God has used me to share this journey with you on how to build a closer relationship with God and discover your true identity, I too had to first experience this for myself. As the saying goes, don't just talk the talk, walk the walk; and let me first start off by saying that this journey has been a life changer for me.

Since 2015, when I started my journey of journaling, praying, fasting, and reading the Word, my life has not been the same. My relationship with God has built my confidence and faith. I decided when I started out that I wanted to have a more intimate relationship with God, and I knew that the closer I would get, the more sacrifices I would have to make. During my journey I found my true strength—and I am not talking about physical strength, but rather spiritual strength, because "God is spirit, and those who worship him must worship in spirit and truth" (John 4:24, ESV). My spiritual strength was elevated to another level. I found that, when studying the Word, it spoke out to me, and it became less challenging for me to understand the scripture as I studied it in my quiet time. My praying was the key that unlocked all the doors to what I wanted, and my prayers became how I would go about receiving it, my habitation.

My constant communication, verbal and written, was what kept me going. I must repeat that again: It was my constant communication, whether verbal or written, that was what kept me from allowing myself to fall prey to Satan. I stood on every word that I could recall in memory. My favorite one that I repeated every day, and even now have placed around my workstation, was Isaiah 55:11 (NKJV). This scripture was the driving force for me to not only complete my journey but also to write the pages you are reading: "So shall my word be that goes forth from my mouth; it shall not return to me void; but it shall accomplish what I please, and it shall prosper in the thing for which I sent it." If God says it, it shall BE!

The next page begins your journaling of your prayer to God for day twenty-nine.

Journal Your Prayer

Day 29

Today's date:_____

Day 30

The Next Level

You are now on the runway, getting ready to take off to the next chapter and next level in your personal relationship with God. You have been in prayer for the past thirty days. This is a significant number; thirty was the age at which Jesus began to minister, teach, and spread the Word of God, and it was through him that we were saved.

Your journey is not completed here; its purpose was to prepare you for your next assignment. I would not have discovered that I was an author, motivator, and prayer warrior had I not continued with building my relationship with God. What you have discovered, and the relationship you have developed with God, has prepared you to move ahead with the opportunity and plan that God has for you. You were created to be set apart and to do the great things he has for you.

Each morning and each night, pray and believe that you can do all things through Christ Jesus, just as Philippians 4:13 (NKJV) says: "I can do all things through Christ who strengthens me." Notice the key term *all*, which means everything, leaving nothing. You don't have to ever doubt or second-guess yourself, you can do all things through Christ Jesus. The other key word in this scripture is *through*. In order to do it, you must come through Christ Jesus; he is your pillar of strength and you can do nothing without him. Stop thinking that you can do it all by yourself; you can only do it with the help of God.

The more you continue to keep open your line of communication with God, the more you will know that God IS anything you can think of. He is the Alpha and the Omega, the Beginning and the End. What God has started, he will finish.

Always remember Philippians 1:6 (KJV), which tells us to "[Be] confident of this very thing, that he which hath begun a good work in you will perform it until the day of Jesus Christ."

The next page begins your journaling of your prayer to God for day thirty.

Journal Your Prayer

Day 30

Today's date:_____

_____
_____
_____
_____
_____
_____
_____
_____
_____
_____
_____
_____
_____
_____

Conclusion

It's never too late to begin the works that God has designed for your life. I never thought that I would become a business owner, author, and speaker all during the course of one year. God has opened up these doors to me and ordered my steps. Whatever the vision and plan God has placed in your spirit, God will perform it. It's up to you to decide if you believe it enough to allow God to use you to accomplish it. We can be our own worst enemy when we allow fear and doubt to overcloud our minds; instead, let this mind be in you that is also in Christ Jesus. Remember, God wants to elevate you and show you all of the plans he has for your life.

The pages you have just finished reading were ordered and designed by the Holy Spirit. It took me exactly fourteen days to complete the first draft of the book you just read. He gave me the words to convey to his people, to you, not only the relationship he wants to have with you, but also, and most importantly, the identity of who you are. God does not want you to walk around in fear and doubt, but in joy and peace. He wants us to experience such abundance that it runs over and fills our neighbors as well.

I challenge you from this point on to continue to develop your relationship with God and allow him to order your steps. In doing this, you will discover the plans and purposes he has for you. It will be a challenge, because the enemy doesn't want you to wake up your spirit. Satan wants you to continue to operate by your own will instead of by the will of God, because once you have surrendered to God's will, look out world, you will be unstoppable!

The plans God has for you are far more than what you can think or imagine for yourself. Stay the course, trust, listen, and obey the steps and plans he will direct for your life.

Let God be your guide. Let me say it again, let God be your guide. It's time for us children of God to walk into our destiny and take back all that the enemy has stolen from us by causing us to doubt. Your visions and dreams will become testimonies to help others, your path will be much brighter, and your enemies will scatter, because you will be walking in the full power and authority that God has placed in your life.

It's time to change your shoes, hold you head up high, and walk with boldness and confidence that God has already spoken in your life. You have dominion and power to speak of any situation or circumstance in your life, even those things that you have not yet performed, as though they have already happened! I call you blessed, women and men of God. Arise and walk into your season!

Blessings,

Melissa Wells

In determining your success one must face all fears and doubts. In accomplishing your success one must know all the strengths and power that lie within!

Melissa Wells, September, 2016

About the Author

Melissa Wells is a first-time author and founder of 2nd Chance Outreach Ministry, Inc., a nonprofit organization where she serves by praying and interceding on behalf of others. She earned her bachelor's degree in business administration from Morris College, followed by her master's degree in health services administration from Strayer University. Melissa is passionate about helping others and spreading the power of prayer. Her central theme in life is that anything is possible with God!

With her children, Raven and Desmond, Melissa lives in Owings Mills, Maryland, where she relaxes by traveling, reading, dancing, and cooking.

To connect, follow Melissa on Twitter @thirtydayprayer.

Amos 3:3

2nd Chance Outreach Ministry, Inc.

"Even YOU deserve a Second Chance"

2nd Chance Outreach Ministry, Inc. is a nonprofit charitable organization that has been designed to help the underprivileged communities in the Baltimore metropolitan and surrounding areas in the state of Maryland. This ministry serves by developing spiritual growth through our connection with social media outlets and prayer lines. Our prayer call line is open to all who are lost and want prayer, for we know that there is power in prayer and that prayer changes things.

For more information about 2nd Chance Outreach Ministry, Inc., you can follow us on Facebook, 2nd Chance Outreach Ministry @ secd2min, and subscribe to us on YouTube, 2nd Chance Ministry.

2nd Chance Outreach Ministry, Inc. Prayer Conference Line

Every Tuesday Night @7pm EST

Telephone: 1-712-775-7085

Access Code: 382039

Playback Recording

Telephone: 1-712-775-7089

Access Code: 382039

purposely created
PUBLISHING

CREATING DISTINCTIVE BOOKS WITH INTENTIONAL RESULTS

We're a collaborative group of creative masterminds with a mission to produce high-quality books to position you for monumental success in the marketplace.

Our professional team of writers, editors, designers, and marketing strategists work closely together to ensure that every detail of your book is a clear representation of the message in your writing.

Want to know more?
Write to us at info@publishyourgift.com
or call (888) 949-6228

Discover great books, exclusive offers, and more at
www.PublishYourGift.com

Connect with us on social media

@publishyourgift

CPSIA information can be obtained
at www.ICGtesting.com
Printed in the USA
FFOW01n2041230518